Bully-Proof

Raising Strong, Confident Kids Who Stand Up for Themselves and Others

Justin Kelly

Bully-Proof: Raising Strong, Confident Kids Who Stand Up for Themselves and Others
Copyright © 2025 Justin Kelly
First Edition Published by Justin Kelly
Second Edition Published by Justin Kelly in Partnership with Butterfly Books Publishing

Cover Design by We Write Books
Photo Credit: Justin Kelly
Interior Design and Typesetting by Butterfly Books Publishing

ISBN (paperback): 978-1-965652-33-6

Printed in the United States of America.

www.bullyproofproject.org
www.butterflybookspublishing.org

Dedication

To my mother, who taught me perseverance when I needed it most. Your strength lives on in me and in the lessons I now pass to others.

To my wife and sons—Mindy, Jared, and Corbin—your love and support mean everything.

Acknowledgments

Thank you to my father, Marvin, and my brother, Jimmy, for always being in my corner.

To my father-in-law, Rick Brooks, for being like a second dad to me.

To my coaches and mentors—Monte Massey, Ron Bausch, Wes Ford, and Grant Leighty—your wisdom and guidance shaped me into the man I am today.

Colson Kipping, a strong young man who's been there with us from the start.

Special thanks to Ironclad Brotherhood, there is great strength in brotherhood!

Table of Contents

Introduction

Growing up, I learned early that the world isn't always kind. There were moments when I felt weak, moments when I doubted myself, and moments when I wished I had the strength to stand up when it mattered most. Over time, through trial, struggle, and a relentless pursuit of growth, I found that strength. I built confidence, learned to fight, and more importantly, learned when not to fight.

As a coach, fighter, and father, I've spent years teaching others how to develop that same confidence—not the kind that comes from empty praise or participation trophies, but real, unshakable confidence built through action, discipline, and resilience. I've seen firsthand how training, mentorship, and the right mindset can transform kids from uncertain and insecure to strong, capable, and ready to face the world.

This book isn't about raising bullies. It's not about teaching kids to be aggressive or to seek out conflict. It's about preparing them—mentally, physically, and emotionally—to navigate a world that isn't always fair. To stand up for themselves and for others. To be the kind of people who tilt the world toward the good.

I've worked with kids who started out timid, afraid of confrontation, and unsure of their place in the world. I've seen them grow, push through discomfort, and come out the other side more confident and prepared for life's challenges. My own sons are examples of this transformation. Through training, discipline, and a commitment to growth, they've become young men who don't just avoid being bullied—they lead, they protect, and they inspire others to do the same.

This book is built on the lessons I've taught in my gym, the principles I've used to guide my own children, and the hard-earned wisdom from years of training and experience. Each chapter will provide practical strategies, real-life examples, and a Parent's Guide at the end to help reinforce these lessons at home.

If you want your child to walk through life with confidence, to stand tall in the face of adversity, and to have the skills to handle themselves when it counts—this book is for you.

Let's raise a generation of bully-proof kids.

Chapter 1
Strength and Confidence – The Foundation of a Bully-Proof Child

Confidence isn't something kids are just born with—it's built. Strength and confidence go hand in hand, and a child who carries themselves with confidence is far less likely to be targeted by bullies. That doesn't mean confidence is about being the biggest or strongest. It means believing in yourself, standing tall, and knowing you can handle what comes your way.

The first step to building confidence is physical. A strong body leads to a strong mind. Kids who train in a sport, especially combat sports like wrestling, jiu-jitsu, or boxing, develop a deep understanding of their own capabilities. They learn they're not fragile. They can take a hit and keep going. And that knowledge doesn't make them aggressive—it makes them calm. They don't feel the need to prove anything to anyone because they know what they're capable of.

Training also teaches kids how to handle adversity. There will be losses, struggles, and moments of doubt, but that's the point. Getting through those tough moments builds resilience. When a child learns to push past discomfort and embrace challenges rather than avoid them, they develop an inner strength that stays with them for life.

A confident child stands differently. They walk with their head up, shoulders back, and eyes alert. This body language alone deters bullies. Bullies look for easy targets—someone who won't fight back, someone who won't speak up. A strong, confident child does not fit that description.

But confidence isn't just about physical training. It's also about knowing how to carry yourself, how to speak up, and how to set boundaries. Kids need to learn that it's okay to say no, that their voice matters, and that they should never feel pressured to do something they're uncomfortable with. This combination of mental and physical confidence is what truly makes a child "bully-proof."

A Real Example: Confidence is Built, Not Given

I've seen it over and over again. Many of my students start off shy, anxious, or unsure of themselves. Some have social anxiety, others have been told they won't develop as quickly as their peers. But in just a few classes, everything changes. Not because they magically become different people, but because they start to earn confidence through preparation and skill-building.

One of my students was told by doctors that his physical development would be much slower than others his age. At first, he was shy and hesitant. But after just a few classes, he was progressing at the same rate as everyone else—maybe even faster in some areas. He worked hard, he pushed through, and eventually, he won our Leader of the Week award, something we give to students who show outstanding improvement and leadership. His growth had nothing to do with natural ability. It was built through effort.

One thing we emphasize above all else is rewarding effort and progress. In our program, confidence isn't about being the toughest—it's about working hard, improving, and pushing yourself. That's why we recognize students who not only develop their own skills but also help others grow. True strength isn't just about standing up for yourself; it's about lifting up those around you.

Every student competes in class, but never in a way that creates division. Competition is friendly, a way to push each other forward, to celebrate growth rather than resent it. Jealousy comes from insecurity, and we eliminate insecurity by making sure every student is prepared and capable. They learn to be genuinely happy for each other's accomplishments, knowing that their own progress will come through effort.

By removing insecurity and replacing it with real skill, we create kids who aren't just bully-proof—they become leaders who inspire others.

Parent's Guide: How to Instill Strength and Confidence in Your Child

As parents, we play a huge role in shaping our children's confidence. Here are a few things you can do to help them develop the strength—both mental and physical—to stand tall against bullies:

Encourage Physical Activity. Whether it's martial arts, team sports, or even just active play, movement builds confidence. Let them struggle and overcome challenges.

Praise Effort, Not Just Talent. When kids are praised for their hard work rather than just their natural ability, they learn that effort leads to success. Instead of saying, "You're so strong," try, "You've been working hard, and it shows."

Teach Assertiveness. Show them how to speak clearly, make eye contact, and stand their ground. Confidence isn't just physical—it's in their voice and posture too.

Let Them Solve Problems. If they come to you with a minor issue, ask, "How do you think you should handle it?" This encourages independence and problem-solving.

Lead by Example. Kids learn from watching us. Carry yourself with confidence, stand up for what's right, and show them what strength looks like in everyday life.

By building their confidence now, you're giving them a gift that will serve them for the rest of their lives. A child who believes in themselves won't just avoid being bullied—they'll be able to stand up for others, face challenges head-on, and grow into a strong, capable adult.

Chapter 2
The Strength in Restraint

Violence is often glorified in movies, sports, and stories of heroism. Strength is frequently mistaken for the ability to dominate others physically. But real strength lies in control—having the power to act but choosing restraint instead.

Many people misunderstand self-defense as simply knowing how to fight. In reality, true self-defense starts with avoiding unnecessary fights altogether. One of the most important lessons a person can learn is that walking away from a confrontation does not make them weak. It makes them wise.

Understanding When to Walk Away

There's a dangerous misconception that backing down means losing. Many young men, especially, feel the need to prove themselves through physical confrontation. But proving yourself isn't about showing how hard you can hit—it's about showing how strong your mind is. When emotions run high, the ability to remain calm and de-escalate a situation is far more valuable than throwing a punch.

I've had my fair share of fights, and I've never regretted the ones I was able to diffuse before they became physical. The regret of fighting when it wasn't necessary is heavy. That's a burden you don't want to carry. Be strong, be unafraid, but show restraint. Your grace will allow your inner peace.

The Power of Confidence

Most fights happen because of insecurity. A person who is truly confident in themselves doesn't feel the need to prove anything to anyone. Training in combat sports or self-defense gives you that confidence—not because it makes you capable of winning a fight, but because it removes the fear of losing one. When you know you can handle yourself, you don't need to seek validation by proving it.

Bullies and aggressors often seek out those they perceive as weak. But weakness isn't just physical—it's also mental. If you stand tall, look people in the eye, and carry yourself with quiet confidence, most threats will pass you by without a second glance.

Strength is in Control

A true warrior knows that fighting is a last resort. Many of the greatest fighters in history, from martial arts masters to world champions, have emphasized restraint as the highest form of discipline. Knowing you could win a fight but choosing not to engage is the ultimate display of power.

This applies beyond physical fights. It's about emotional and mental battles, too. Resisting the urge to lash out when angry, walking away from arguments that don't serve you, and maintaining control in the face of provocation—these are all marks of true strength.

The Consequences of Unnecessary Violence

Every action has consequences. Even if you win a fight, there may be legal, social, or emotional repercussions. A single moment of unchecked aggression can lead to a lifetime of regret. Many fighters and self-defense experts will tell you that fighting should always be the last option because once it starts, the outcome is unpredictable.

I've had fights where I defended myself, but in the heat of the moment, I took it further than necessary. Those moments haunt me. The guilt of knowing I could have stopped sooner weighs heavier than any physical damage I've ever taken. We must always remember that the goal of self-defense is not to punish—it's to protect.

The Path to Mastery

Training in self-defense, martial arts, or combat sports isn't just about learning how to fight—it's about learning when not to. The best fighters in the world don't go looking for trouble. They walk away because they know they don't need to prove anything to anyone.

If you are training, do so with the mindset that your skills are for protection, not aggression. A well-trained fighter has nothing to prove. They are not reckless with their strength because they understand its value.

Final Thoughts

Real strength isn't about how hard you hit—it's about how much control you have over yourself. Walking away doesn't make you weak; it makes you disciplined. Knowing when to act and when to stand down is the mark of true confidence. Your goal should never be to fight, but to live with the peace of knowing that if the time comes, you are ready—but only if there is no other way.

Self-defense isn't just about survival; it's about ensuring you can live your life with confidence, integrity, and peace of mind. The greatest victories are the battles you never have to fight.

Parent's Guide: Teaching Strength Through Restraint

As parents, we want our kids to be strong, but strength isn't just about standing up for themselves—it's about knowing when to walk away. Here's how you can help your child develop self-control, confidence, and the wisdom to avoid unnecessary conflict:

1. Model Emotional Control

Kids learn more from what we do than what we say. If they see us staying calm in difficult situations, they'll understand that real strength is in self-control. Make it a rule to never discipline when you're angry—wait until you can guide them, not react emotionally.

2. Teach That Walking Away is Strength, Not Weakness

Many kids, especially boys, believe that backing down is losing. Explain to them that true strength is in control, not aggression. Share stories of people who avoided fights and made the right choice.

3. Encourage Assertiveness Over Aggression

Assertiveness means standing your ground with confidence—without hostility. Teach them to:

- Speak clearly and firmly.
- Make eye contact.
- Set boundaries without anger.

4. Role-Play Conflict Resolution

Kids sometimes struggle with knowing how to walk away. Practice scenarios where they:

- Stay calm when someone insults them.

- Use humor or confidence to defuse a tense situation.

- Recognize when a fight isn't worth it.

5. Reinforce That Strength is for Protection, Not Power

If your child trains in martial arts or self-defense, remind them that their skills are not for proving themselves—they are for protecting themselves and others when absolutely necessary.

By teaching restraint, we're not just keeping our kids safe from fights—they're also learning discipline, patience, and self-respect, which will benefit them for life.

Chapter 3
Strength and Confidence Through Physical Training

One of the most effective ways to bully-proof a child is by developing their strength and confidence through physical training. This doesn't mean raising a child to be aggressive or to seek conflict, but rather equipping them with the tools to carry themselves with assurance and resilience. A child who is physically capable and confident in their abilities is far less likely to be targeted by bullies, and they are also more likely to stand up for others when needed.

The Connection Between Strength and Confidence

Confidence is often rooted in capability. When a child knows they can defend themselves, they walk with a different energy—one that doesn't invite confrontation. This isn't about teaching kids to fight; it's about teaching them to handle themselves. Wrestling, martial arts, and combat sports instill not only physical skills but also discipline, respect, and self-control.

I've seen this transformation firsthand. Kids who enter my classes timid and unsure of themselves begin to change within weeks.

Their posture improves, they start making eye contact, and they become more vocal in group settings. This isn't because they've been taught to be aggressive, but because they've discovered their own strength. They no longer feel powerless, and that shift is everything.

Why Physical Training Matters

The unfortunate reality is that kids who appear weak or uncertain are often the first targets of bullies. Predators look for easy prey. A child who looks unsure of themselves, who averts their eyes, and who slouches when they walk is signaling vulnerability. Physical training changes that. A child who is strong, fit, and confident in their body language becomes a far less appealing target.

Beyond protection, there's also an internal transformation. Strength training, wrestling, and martial arts force kids to push past their perceived limits. They learn that they are capable of more than they thought, and that lesson carries over into every aspect of life. When a child overcomes a tough workout, survives a difficult sparring session, or finally masters a new technique, they internalize a simple truth:

"I can do hard things."

The Importance of Making It Fun

Physical training should never feel like a punishment. The key to long-term success is making it enjoyable. The best way to get kids excited about training is to incorporate games, challenges, and friendly competition. In my classes, we mix skill-building drills with fun activities that keep kids engaged while reinforcing the fundamentals of movement, agility, and strength. When kids enjoy what they're doing, they're far more likely to stick with it, and consistency is what builds real confidence.

My own sons are great examples of this. They didn't start training because they wanted to be fighters; they started because it was fun. Over time, their skills grew, and so did their confidence. They weren't the biggest kids in school, but they were among the most respected. Why? Because they carried themselves with an unshakable confidence that only comes from knowing you can handle yourself if needed.

Teaching Controlled Strength

Strength without control is dangerous. It's crucial that as kids grow physically stronger, they also develop the maturity to use that strength responsibly. This is something we emphasize in every class. Just because you can win a fight doesn't mean you should fight.

I've had my own experiences where I went too far in a fight and regretted it afterward. The power to hurt someone comes with the responsibility not to. That's why every lesson in strength is paired with a lesson in restraint. True confidence doesn't come from proving your dominance—it comes from knowing you don't have to.

Building a Foundation for Life

The lessons learned through physical training go far beyond self-defense. Kids who train develop discipline, patience, and a work ethic that serves them in school, sports, and life. They understand that effort leads to improvement and that persistence pays off. These are invaluable life skills that extend far beyond the gym.

By teaching kids to be physically capable, we are giving them the ability to walk through life without fear. A confident child is a child who can stand tall in the face of adversity, who can say "no" to peer pressure, and who can be a leader among their peers. This chapter isn't just about self-defense; it's about setting kids up for success in every aspect of life.

Key Takeaways

- Physical training builds confidence, resilience, and self-discipline.

- Strength and proper body language reduce the likelihood of being targeted by bullies.

- Training should be fun and engaging to keep kids motivated.

- Strength must always be paired with responsibility and restraint.

- The lessons learned through physical training extend far beyond self-defense.

- A bully-proof child isn't just strong in body—they're strong in mind and character. Physical training is simply the foundation on which that strength is built.

Parent's Guide: How to Encourage Strength and Confidence Through Training

As parents, we have the power to shape our children's relationship with physical activity, discipline, and self-confidence. Here's how to ensure they get the most out of training:

1. Make Physical Activity a Normal Part of Life

Encourage movement every day—whether it's sports, play, or structured training.

Be active as a family. Go for hikes, bike rides, or play games that involve movement.

Show them that staying strong and healthy is a lifelong practice, not just something for kids.

2. Help Them Find the Right Activity

Not every child is drawn to the same type of training. Some may love wrestling or jiu-jitsu, while others may prefer traditional martial arts, gymnastics, or strength training. The key is to help them find something they enjoy so they stick with it.

3. Praise Effort Over Natural Ability

Kids need to learn that improvement comes from consistent effort, not just talent. Instead of saying, "You're so strong!" try:

"I can tell you've been working hard."

"That move looked smoother than last time—you're improving!"

This teaches them that success is in their control and encourages them to keep pushing themselves.

4. Teach Responsibility Alongside Strength

With physical strength comes responsibility. Reinforce that their training isn't about hurting others but about discipline, self-respect, and protection.

5. Lead by Example

If you value fitness, self-discipline, and perseverance, your child will see it. Show them through your actions that taking care of your body and pushing through challenges is a lifelong practice.

6. Encourage a Growth Mindset

If they struggle, remind them that challenges are how we improve.

Help them set small goals—like mastering a new skill or improving their endurance—and celebrate their progress.

Teach them that failure isn't a sign to quit but a lesson on how to get better.

7. Keep It Fun

No matter how serious training is, kids need to enjoy it. Encourage their instructors to incorporate games and challenges. Let them compete, but make sure they know that progress matters more than winning.

By making physical training a part of their life—one that's enjoyable, rewarding, and full of growth—you're helping them develop a mindset that will serve them well beyond childhood. A confident, capable child is a child who will walk through life with strength, resilience, and the courage to stand tall.

Chapter 4
Avoiding Confrontation

One of the most important skills in self-defense has nothing to do with fighting—it's learning how to avoid a fight altogether. Many people, especially kids, feel like they have something to prove. They think walking away makes them look weak, but in reality, it's the smartest and strongest choice in most situations.

Why Avoiding a Fight is Not Weakness

There's a dangerous myth that backing down means you're scared. The truth is, real strength comes from knowing you could fight but choosing not to. Walking away doesn't mean you're afraid; it means you're smart enough to see the bigger picture. A fight should only happen when there is absolutely no other choice.

Some of the toughest fighters in the world will tell you they avoid fights in public. Why? Because they know the consequences:

Getting into a fight can lead to injuries, sometimes severe or even life-altering.

There could be legal trouble—even if you were defending yourself.

Even if you win, you might regret the outcome.

I've had fights where I defended myself, and while I don't regret protecting myself, I do regret situations where I let my emotions take over when I didn't need to. Teaching kids that it's okay to walk away can save them from unnecessary trouble.

Reading a Situation Before It Escalates

A big part of avoiding confrontation is awareness. Many fights can be avoided if you recognize warning signs early. Here are some things kids should learn to watch for:

- Body language – Someone standing too close, clenching their fists, puffing their chest, or making aggressive gestures.

- Verbal escalation – Name-calling, taunts, or threats.

- A shift in tone – If someone suddenly changes from joking to serious, it's a warning sign that things might escalate.

If you see these signs, the best move is to get out of the situation before it turns physical. There's no shame in leaving if you sense trouble coming.

The One Warning Rule

In my classes, I teach kids a one warning rule for situations where they can't just walk away:

"I don't want to do this, but if you try to hurt me again, I'm going to defend myself."

This approach does two things:

1. It gives the other person a chance to stop – Sometimes, people are acting tough but don't actually want a fight.

2. It mentally prepares the defender – If a fight is unavoidable, they've already set their boundary and are ready to act.

One Warning Doesn't Mean You Have to Get Hit

Some people misinterpret the idea of "giving a warning" as meaning they have to take a hit first. That's absolutely not the case. If someone is already making an obvious attempt to hit you—if they're throwing a punch or lunging at you—you have every right to defend yourself immediately.

I hate the phrase "You have to take the first punch." That kind of thinking can be disastrous. Taking a direct hit can leave you dazed or even knock you out. If someone is attacking you, you do not have to let them land the first strike—you have the right to protect yourself before that happens.

The warning is about giving them a chance to back down, not about letting yourself get hurt. If it's clear that they aren't stopping, you have to act decisively to defend yourself.

Confidence and Control

Many fights start because of ego, not real danger. When kids have confidence, they don't feel the need to prove themselves. That's why training matters—it removes insecurity. When a child knows they can defend themselves, they don't have to seek out fights or respond to every challenge.

I've seen kids in my classes go from shy and nervous to standing tall and unshaken in tough situations. When you feel strong, you don't let other people's words control you. Bullies feed off reactions, and when they don't get one, they usually lose interest.

When Walking Away is Not an Option

While avoidance is the best strategy, there are moments when a fight might be unavoidable:

If someone physically attacks you and you have no way to escape.

If someone is trying to hurt someone else, and you have to step in to protect them.

If you're cornered with no safe way to leave.

This is where training kicks in. The goal isn't to fight—it's to end the threat as quickly as possible and get to safety.

Final Thoughts

Avoiding confrontation isn't about being afraid; it's about being smart. A truly strong person knows when to walk away and when to stand their ground. Teaching kids to be aware of danger, to set clear boundaries, and to act decisively when necessary can prevent a lot of unnecessary fights—and keep them safe when a fight is unavoidable.

Parent's Guide: Teaching Kids to Avoid Unnecessary Fights

Avoiding confrontation is just as much a learned skill as self-defense itself. As parents, we play a big role in shaping how our kids handle conflict.

What You Can Do:

Talk About the Power of Walking Away – Help kids understand that avoiding a fight is a sign of strength, not weakness. Share stories of athletes, role models, or personal experiences where walking away was the better choice.

Teach Them to Identify Warning Signs – Encourage your child to recognize aggressive body language, verbal threats, and escalating situations so they can remove themselves before things get physical.

Role-Play Scenarios – Practice different situations where they might be challenged, and help them come up with confident, non-aggressive ways to de-escalate.

Set the Example – Kids learn by watching. If they see parents or role models handling conflict with calm and confidence rather than aggression, they'll do the same.

Make Sure They Understand Self-Defense Laws – While kids should know they can defend themselves, they should also understand the difference between self-defense and starting a fight. Make sure they know that legally and morally, their goal should always be to stop a threat and get to safety—not to prove a point.

What to Emphasize:

"One Warning" doesn't mean letting yourself get hit.

Confidence and presence can prevent most fights before they start.

Knowing how to fight makes you less likely to need to fight.

Being strong enough to walk away is real power.

By giving our kids the tools to recognize danger, set boundaries, and act with confidence, we're helping them navigate the world with strength and intelligence.

Chapter 5
When Walking Away Isn't an Option

Avoiding conflict is always the best choice when possible. A smart fighter knows that the best way to win a fight is to never be in one. But there are times when walking away isn't an option. When someone is intent on harming you, when there's no escape, or when protecting yourself or others is necessary—this is when self-defense becomes essential.

Understanding Real Danger

Not every confrontation requires a fight, but recognizing the difference between a threat and posturing is a critical skill. Some people act tough to intimidate but have no real intent to attack. Others are looking for an excuse to lash out.

Signs that a fight is imminent:

- The person invades your personal space aggressively.

- They clench their fists or shift their weight like they're preparing to strike.

- They glance around to see if anyone is watching—checking for witnesses.

- They try to corner you or cut off your ability to leave.

- Their face shows clear aggression—tight jaw, flared nostrils, eyes locked on you.

When you see these signs, your priority should still be to de-escalate or escape if possible. But if it's clear they're about to attack, you must be ready to defend yourself.

One Warning—But No Hesitation

One of the most important principles I teach my students is One Warning. If someone is getting aggressive, you don't have to let them hit you first. That's one of the most dangerous myths out there.

Your warning should be clear, firm, and loud enough that witnesses can hear:

"I don't want to do this, but if you try to hurt me, I will defend myself."

This isn't about being polite—it's about showing confidence and creating a record of your intent. If someone is set on harming you, they will ignore the warning, but it sets a boundary and gives you the moral and legal justification to defend yourself.

You do NOT have to wait to get hit. If someone makes an obvious attempt to hit you—whether they throw a punch, grab you, or make a clear move toward violence—you have the right to strike first to protect yourself.

Preemptive Self-Defense

The term "taking the first punch" is misleading and dangerous. In reality, striking first can be the difference between winning and losing a fight. If an aggressor has made it clear they are going to attack, allowing them to land the first blow could put you in a position where you can't fight back effectively.

Preemptive self-defense means acting the moment you know an attack is inevitable. This isn't about throwing a punch out of fear—it's about neutralizing the threat before they can hurt you.

Controlled Aggression

Once a fight begins, your goal is to end it as quickly as possible. Self-defense is not about exchanging punches like in a boxing match—it's about survival. Every strike should have a purpose:

- **Target vulnerabilities** – Eyes, nose, throat, knees, groin.

- **Use explosive movements** – Fast, aggressive counterattacks overwhelm most attackers.

- **Stay on your feet** – If you go to the ground, get up fast unless you're trained in ground fighting.

- **Control distance** – If they're bigger, keep space. If they're slower, close the gap.

The Mental Side of Fighting

A fight isn't just physical—it's mental. Fear can either paralyze you or fuel you. The key is controlling your adrenaline. Breathe, stay calm, and trust your training. The more prepared you are, the less fear will control you.

I tell my students: "If you've trained hard, your body already knows what to do. Your job is to stay calm and let it happen."

After the Fight

If you've had to defend yourself, leave the area as soon as it's safe. Call a trusted person and, if necessary, report the incident. If authorities are involved, be clear that you acted in self-defense. Never brag about winning a fight—your goal was survival, not proving anything.

Parent's Guide: Teaching Kids When and How to Defend Themselves

As parents, we want our kids to be safe, but we also want them to know how to stand up for themselves when necessary. Here's how to help them understand when and how to act in dangerous situations.

1. Make It Clear That Violence Is a Last Resort

Kids should understand that fighting isn't about winning—it's about protection. Reinforce that walking away is always the best option when possible, but some situations require action.

2. Teach the Signs of Danger

Go over body language cues and warning signs of aggression. Help them recognize when someone is just trying to scare them versus when they are truly in danger.

3. Give Them a Simple Plan

Kids need clear instructions. Teach them:

- **Step back and raise your hands** – This signals they don't want to fight but prepares them to defend.

- **Use a firm voice** – A strong verbal warning can sometimes stop a fight before it starts.

- **Defend immediately if attacked** – No hesitation. If they're being grabbed or swung at, they must act fast.

4. Emphasize Control and Responsibility

Make sure they understand that self-defense doesn't mean hurting someone more than necessary. Their goal is to stop the threat, not punish the attacker.

5. Keep Open Communication

If your child is ever involved in a fight, make sure they know they can talk to you without fear of punishment if they acted in self-defense. Help them process what happened and reinforce the lessons learned.

Key Takeaways for Parents:

- Fighting is a last resort, but knowing when to act is crucial.
- Kids should recognize warning signs of real danger.
- They should never let an attacker hit them first if a fight is unavoidable.
- Controlled aggression is necessary for self-defense.
- Always encourage open communication after a confrontation.

A child who knows they have the ability to defend themselves carries confidence that extends into all areas of life. By preparing them mentally and physically, we ensure they never feel powerless.

Chapter 6
Peer Pressure and Social Dynamics

Peer pressure is one of the biggest challenges kids face. It doesn't always come in the form of bullying—it can be subtle, even disguised as friendship. The desire to fit in is natural, but knowing when to resist the crowd is a skill that sets strong individuals apart.

Understanding Peer Pressure

Peer pressure isn't always direct. It can be:

Spoken – Someone dares you to do something or calls you names if you don't.

Unspoken – You feel like you have to act a certain way to be accepted.

Positive – A good friend pushes you to study harder or train harder.

Negative – Someone pressures you to break rules or go against your values.

Recognizing these influences is the first step to handling them effectively.

The Power of "No"

One of the most valuable skills a person can learn is how to say "no" with confidence. It doesn't have to be aggressive, but it must be firm.

Ways to say no without inviting more pressure:

- The Casual No – "Nah, I'm good."

- The Confident No – "I don't do that."

- The Redirect – "That's not my thing, let's do something else."

- The Humor Approach – "Yeah, because that worked out great for the last guy who tried it."

Confidence is key. Most of the time, the people applying pressure will move on if they see you're not easy to manipulate.

Choosing the Right Circle

The people you surround yourself with will shape your future. Strong friendships should be built on respect, not pressure. If someone only likes you when you follow their lead, they're not a real friend.

A strong peer group will:

- ✓ Support your goals

- ✓ Respect your boundaries

- ✓ Encourage you to improve

- ✓ Have your back when things get tough

A weak peer group will:

- ✗ Pressure you into bad decisions

- ✗ Mock you for making the right choice

- ✗ Abandon you when you need them most

- ✗ Tear you down instead of lifting you up

Who you spend time with is one of the biggest factors in your success or failure. Choose wisely.

Standing Alone Is Better Than Standing with the Wrong Crowd

Many kids fear that standing up for themselves will leave them isolated. The truth is, standing alone for what's right attracts real respect. It might take time, but strong people gravitate toward others who show strength.

Tilting the World the Right Way

Every day, we make choices that affect the world around us. We either tilt it toward the good or the bad. The way we treat people, the way we stand up for others, and the way we resist negative influence all matter.

One of the most powerful things I tell my students:

"Every day when we wake up, we have a choice to make. We have an effect on the world, whether we realize it or not, and that effect is more important than we realize. We're either tilting the world to the good or to the bad. Make sure you're tilting the world the right way. However big your effect is, make sure it's making the world a better place—not worse."

Parent's Guide: Helping Kids Handle Peer Pressure

As parents, we can't always control who our kids encounter, but we can prepare them to make the right choices.

1. Teach Them to Recognize Peer Pressure

Explain that peer pressure isn't always obvious. Sometimes, it's as subtle as a friend making them feel dumb for saying no. Helping them identify it early gives them the ability to resist it.

2. Build Their Confidence in Decision-Making

A child who is used to making decisions won't be easily influenced. Give them opportunities to make choices, even in small ways, so they learn to trust their judgment.

3. Reinforce That Saying "No" Is a Strength, Not a Weakness

Make sure they understand that standing their ground isn't something to be ashamed of. Role-playing different scenarios can help them practice their responses.

4. Encourage Strong, Positive Friendships

Help them recognize the difference between a real friend and someone who just wants control. Encourage activities where they can meet like-minded kids.

5. Keep the Communication Open

Kids need to know they can talk to you without fear of judgment. Make it clear that they won't get in trouble for telling the truth about situations they've faced.

Key Takeaways for Parents:

- Help kids recognize different types of peer pressure.
- Build their confidence in making their own choices.
- Teach them that "no" is a powerful tool.
- Encourage friendships based on mutual respect.
- Keep communication open so they feel safe coming to you.

A child who can resist negative peer pressure grows into an adult who makes strong, independent choices. Teaching this early is one of the best gifts we can give them.

Chapter 7: Leadership, Accountability, and Integrity

One of the most important things we can teach kids is that they have a responsibility to make the world a better place. Strength, confidence, and resilience are important—but without accountability and integrity, they mean nothing.

A truly bully-proof kid isn't just someone who can defend themselves. It's someone who lifts others up, takes responsibility for their actions, and stands firm in their values, even when no one is watching.

Leadership Starts with Responsibility

Being a leader isn't about giving orders or being the loudest in the room. It's about taking responsibility—for yourself and for those around you. True leadership starts with personal accountability.

A strong leader:

- ✓ Sets the right example, even when no one is watching.

- ✓ Takes ownership of their mistakes instead of blaming others.

✓ Speaks up when something is wrong, even when it's hard.

✓ Treats others with respect and never abuses power.

One of the biggest lessons I try to instill in my students is this: You don't have to be in charge to be a leader. Leadership is about how you carry yourself and the choices you make.

Integrity: Doing the Right Thing When It's Hard

Integrity means doing what's right—even when it's inconvenient, even when no one will ever know. A person with integrity doesn't take shortcuts, doesn't betray their values, and doesn't mistreat people just because they can.

Kids who develop integrity early will grow into adults who don't fall apart under pressure, who don't sell out their morals for approval, and who don't let fear stop them from making the right choices.

Accountability: Owning Your Actions

In today's world, people love to make excuses. But the strongest individuals are the ones who take ownership of their actions.

If you mess up, admit it.

If you hurt someone, make it right.

If you want something, work for it.

The moment a kid learns to take full accountability for their actions is the moment they step into real strength. Excuses are easy—growth is hard. But growth is what builds true confidence.

Tilting the World the Right Way

I tell my students this often:

"Every day when we wake up, we have a choice to make. We have an effect on the world, whether we realize it or not, and that effect is more important than we realize. We're either tilting the world to the good or to the bad. Make sure you're tilting the world the right way. However big your effect is, make sure it's making the world a better place—not worse."

That choice is the foundation of leadership. If we want to raise kids who make the world better, we have to teach them that their actions matter—every single day.

Parent's Guide: Teaching Leadership, Accountability, and Integrity

1. Give Kids Real Responsibility

Kids need opportunities to be responsible. Give them tasks that matter—things they can take pride in. Whether it's taking care of a pet, helping a younger sibling, or being in charge of a household chore, real responsibility builds real confidence.

2. Model Accountability

Kids learn by watching. If they see you owning your mistakes and holding yourself to a high standard, they'll do the same. If they see excuses and blame, they'll pick that up instead.

3. Praise Effort and Integrity, Not Just Success

Kids need to know that how they achieve something matters just as much as achieving it. If they cheat to win, that's not a victory. If they do the right thing even when it costs them, that's a real win.

4. Teach Them to Speak Up

One of the hardest things to do is stand up for what's right—especially when you're standing alone. Encourage your child to be the kind of person who speaks up when something is wrong, even if it's uncomfortable.

5. Reinforce That Their Actions Matter

Kids sometimes feel like they're too small to make a difference. Remind them that every choice they make, every interaction they have, and every person they help has an impact.

Key Takeaways for Parents:

- Give kids real responsibilities to build leadership skills.
- Model accountability by owning your own mistakes.
- Praise effort, hard work, and integrity—not just results.
- Encourage them to speak up for what's right.
- Reinforce that their actions have an impact on the world.

Raising a child with leadership, accountability, and integrity means raising a child who will stand strong in the face of life's challenges. And that's the ultimate goal—not just to protect them from bullies, but to prepare them for life.

Chapter 8
Mental Resilience and Overcoming Fear

Fear is a natural part of life. Every child will face fear at some point—fear of failure, fear of rejection, fear of standing alone. The difference between a confident, bully-proof child and a vulnerable one isn't the absence of fear—it's their ability to face it and push through.

Mental resilience is the foundation of real strength. It's what allows a child to keep going when things get hard, to stand firm when others waver, and to hold onto their values even when the world is pressuring them to fold.

Understanding Fear: It's Not the Enemy

Fear isn't the enemy—it's a signal. It's our body and mind telling us that we're stepping into something difficult or unfamiliar. The key isn't to eliminate fear, but to learn how to respond to it.

A mentally tough child doesn't let fear control their actions. Instead, they acknowledge it, assess the situation, and decide their next move with a clear head. That's the difference between someone who freezes under pressure and someone who rises to the challenge.

Building Resilience Through Challenge

Resilience doesn't come from comfort—it comes from struggle. A child who never faces challenges won't develop the ability to push through when things get tough.

That's why I believe in pushing kids past their comfort zones. Whether it's through physical training, competition, or simply encouraging them to step up in difficult moments, they need to learn that they can do hard things.

I've seen this firsthand in training. A kid gets put in a tough spot— a bad position in a grappling match, exhaustion setting in during a drill, or fear creeping in before a sparring session. If they push through, something changes in them. They realize that their mind will quit before their body does, and that they are far more capable than they thought. That's the foundation of real confidence.

The Power of Staying Calm Under Pressure

One of the biggest lessons in resilience is learning to stay calm in difficult situations. When kids panic, they make bad decisions. But when they train their minds to stay level-headed, they can think clearly even in high-stress moments.

I've had my own moments where staying calm made the difference between success and failure.

I once escaped a deep guillotine choke in a fight by focusing on staying calm and thinking in short time frames—one breath at a time, one small movement at a time.

I took a brutal knee to the solar plexus in a title fight. I couldn't breathe, but I forced myself to stay composed and rely on my training instead of panicking.

I've been in real-life situations where my ability to keep a clear head kept me safe.

These lessons don't just apply to fights. They apply to life. A child who learns to stay calm under pressure will be able to handle bullies, peer pressure, and life's toughest moments with confidence.

Teaching Kids to Face Fear Instead of Avoiding It

Too many parents try to shield their kids from discomfort, but that only makes them weaker. Kids need to learn to face fear and push through it.

Here's what I teach my students:

- If something scares you, don't avoid it—lean into it.

- The only way to get over fear is by proving to yourself that you can handle it.

- Small victories over fear add up. Every time you push through, you get stronger.

The Strength to Keep Going

Life is going to throw challenges at every child. Some will crumble. Some will keep going. The ones who keep going are the ones who learn mental resilience early.

One of the hardest things my own sons ever went through was losing loved ones—their grandmother, and later, their two best friends at the same time in an unexplainable tragedy. They had every reason to shut down, to give up. But they didn't. They leaned on each other, they leaned on their training, and they found the strength to push forward.

That's what resilience looks like. Not pretending things don't hurt, but refusing to let them break you.

Parent's Guide: Teaching Mental Resilience and Overcoming Fear

1. Let Kids Struggle (Within Reason)

Struggle is how resilience is built. Let your kids face challenges instead of rescuing them every time. Whether it's a tough test, a difficult sport, or an uncomfortable social situation, let them work through it.

2. Teach Them to Control Their Reactions

Help kids learn to slow down and breathe when they're scared or overwhelmed. The ability to stay calm under pressure is one of the most valuable skills they can develop.

3. Praise Effort, Not Just Success

The goal isn't to avoid failure—it's to keep going despite it. Praise your child when they push through a tough moment, even if they don't win. The lesson is in the effort.

4. Encourage Facing Fear in Small Steps

If a child is afraid of something, help them tackle it in small, manageable steps. Fear shrinks when you face it little by little.

5. Be the Example

Your kids will learn resilience from watching you more than from anything you tell them. If they see you handle stress with a clear head, take ownership of your challenges, and keep moving forward when life gets tough, they'll learn to do the same.

Key Takeaways for Parents:

- Let kids struggle—it builds resilience.
- Teach them to control their reactions in tough moments.
- Praise effort and perseverance, not just results.
- Help them face fear in small, manageable steps.
- Model resilience in your own life.

Mental resilience is the difference between a child who breaks under pressure and a child who rises above it. Teach them now, and they'll carry that strength for life.

Chapter 9
Mastering Fear and Preparedness

The Power of Preparedness

Fear is natural. It's a survival instinct meant to keep us alive. But if you let it control you, it will make you weak. The difference between those who freeze in fear and those who act is preparation.

Prepared people don't panic. They don't hesitate. They react because they've already faced the situation in their mind a hundred times before it happens.

Mastering fear doesn't mean you never feel it—it means you control it instead of letting it control you.

Fear Is Just an Illusion

Fear feels real in the moment. Your heart pounds. Your mind races. You feel like you're drowning in it.

But here's the truth: fear is just an illusion. It only has as much power as you give it. The key to overcoming fear is action. The second you start moving, fear starts fading.

Think about the first time you sparred, the first time you stepped into a competition, or even the first time you spoke in front of a crowd. The fear leading up to it was worse than the moment itself. Once you engaged, your training took over. That's how it works in life, too.

Fear loses its grip the second you take control.

Staying Calm Under Pressure

The most dangerous situations aren't just about strength—they're about mental toughness. If you can't control your fear, you can't make smart decisions.

Here's what I teach my students about staying calm under pressure:

- **Control your breathing** – If you panic, your breathing gets shallow. Slow it down, take deep breaths, and force yourself to stay in control.

- **Shorten your focus** – Don't think about everything at once. Just focus on what you can do right now.

- **Act, don't freeze** – The first move you make can shift the fight in your favor. When the time comes, don't hesitate.

Real-Life Examples of Staying Calm Under Fire

The Guillotine Choke Escape

I was caught in a deep guillotine choke once, and the instinct would've been to panic, to thrash, to waste energy. But I stayed calm. I shortened my focus. First, I stopped the choke from getting tighter. Then, inch by inch, I created space, found the right angle, and escaped.

If I had panicked, I would've tapped. Instead, I turned a bad situation into a win.

The Knee to the Solar Plexus

I remember a title fight where I took a brutal knee to the solar plexus. It knocked the wind out of me, and for a split second, my body wanted to fold. But I didn't let it. I kept my posture, hid my reaction, and acted like it didn't bother me.

My opponent thought he hadn't landed clean, so he didn't press the attack. That gave me just enough time to recover, and I won the fight.

These moments weren't about strength alone. They were about mental control—about knowing that fear and pain don't have to dictate your actions.

Never Make Fear-Based Decisions

In the moment of chaos and fear, never make fear-based decisions. Slow your mind, shorten your focus, and find the solution.

If you're attacked by someone bigger, stronger, or more experienced, remember: you don't have to win the fight—you just have to change his mind.

A sudden, hard strike to the chin can make him rethink. A quick escape can throw him off. The fight is won in the mind as much as the body.

Be Ready for the Unexpected

If there's one thing I've learned, it's that nothing goes exactly how you plan it. Something strange or unpredictable always happens. Be ready to change your plan in the middle of the action.

- Have a plan—but don't be shocked when it changes.

- Stay adaptable. Good decision-making under pressure is how you survive.

- The people who get through bad situations are the ones who can think while others panic.

Preparedness Is the Key to Confidence

Confidence doesn't come from faking it. It comes from knowing you're prepared.

The more prepared you are, the calmer you'll be when things go wrong. Whether it's a fight, an emergency, or any high-stakes situation, the person who stays in control is the one who wins.

Preparedness kills fear. It turns hesitation into action. It gives you the power to make the right decisions when it matters most.

Parent's Guide: Helping Kids Master Fear

Teach them to recognize fear but not be controlled by it. Fear is natural, but action overcomes it.

Use real-life examples to show how staying calm leads to success. Sports, self-defense, and problem-solving all reinforce this.

Help them practice decision-making under pressure. Games and drills where they have to think fast help build confidence.

Talk about mental toughness. Kids need to hear that staying calm is a skill they can develop, not just something they're born with.

Make preparedness a habit. From self-defense to handling emergencies, kids who train for challenges don't freeze when they face them.

Chapter 10
The Strength in Silence

True Strength Isn't Loud

The strongest people in the world don't need to announce it. They don't need to brag, show off, or try to prove anything to anyone. That's because real confidence comes from knowing what you're capable of—not from needing others to see it.

Think about the loudest people in the room. The ones who talk the biggest game. The ones who feel the need to puff out their chests and act tough. More often than not, they're the easiest to defeat. Why? Because they rely on image, not substance. Their confidence is a show, and when that show gets challenged, they crumble.

The strongest men in history—the ones who truly made an impact—didn't waste time trying to impress people with words. They let their actions speak for them.

The Loudest Ones Are the Weakest

The biggest talkers usually have the most to prove. And when someone has something to prove, they're acting out of insecurity.

They need people to believe they're strong because, deep down, they don't fully believe it themselves.

In my years of training, I've fought plenty of guys who ran their mouths. The ones who swore they were unbeatable. The ones who bragged about their power. And time after time, those were the easiest fights. They weren't focused. They weren't prepared. They thought talking tough was enough—but when it came down to it, they didn't have the discipline, skill, or resilience to back it up.

On the other hand, the guys who walked in quietly, who didn't feel the need to put on a show—those were the ones you had to watch out for. They weren't looking for approval. They weren't trying to scare you. They were just there to do what needed to be done.

Teaching Kids the Power of Quiet Confidence

Kids today are surrounded by noise. Social media, peer pressure, and the constant need for validation make it seem like you have to be loud to be important. But that's not true.

A child who learns quiet confidence early in life is unstoppable. They don't waste energy trying to prove themselves to the wrong people. They don't feel the need to show off or get the last word. They carry themselves in a way that commands respect—without ever having to demand it.

We need to teach kids:

- Strength isn't about being the loudest—it's about being the most prepared.

- Great men don't need to brag. They let their actions speak.

- The biggest talkers are usually the weakest fighters.

- Confidence is quiet. Insecurity is loud.

When a child understands this, they gain a huge advantage in life. They learn to see past the noise. They recognize that real strength doesn't come from proving yourself—it comes from knowing yourself.

The Power of Silence in Conflict

One of the most effective ways to de-escalate a situation is to refuse to engage with nonsense.

When someone tries to bait you into a fight—verbally or physically—the best response is often no response at all. Silence is powerful. It makes people uncomfortable. It forces them to confront their own insecurities. It takes away their ability to control you.

When a bully is looking for a reaction and they don't get one, they lose interest. When someone's trying to intimidate you and you remain calm, they start second-guessing themselves. And if the situation does turn physical, the person who conserved their energy and stayed composed has the upper hand every time.

Final Thoughts: Be the One They Respect, Not the One They Hear

A truly strong person doesn't seek attention. They don't waste words trying to impress people. They don't let their ego run their decisions.

Instead, they prepare. They train. They stay disciplined. And when the time comes, they act with precision and purpose.

The world is full of noise, but the ones who make the biggest impact are the ones who don't need to be loud. They just do what needs to be done.

Parent's Guide: Teaching Kids Quiet Confidence

Encourage self-discipline. Confidence grows from competence. The more kids develop their skills, the less they feel the need to prove themselves.

Lead by example. If you don't need to talk about how strong or successful you are, they'll learn to do the same.

Teach them to recognize insecurity. When kids understand that the loudest people are often the weakest, they stop being intimidated by big talkers.

Show them the power of silence. Teach them that not every challenge requires a response. Sometimes, the best way to win is by refusing to play the game.

A child who learns quiet confidence will grow into a strong, respected adult. And that's the real goal—not to be the loudest, but to be the most prepared.

Chapter 11
The Protector's Mindset – Becoming a Guardian for Others

The ultimate goal of everything in this book—self-defense, confidence, leadership—is to raise kids who become protectors. A bully-proof kid isn't just someone who can stand up for themselves. They're someone who stands up for others.

I've seen it time and time again: kids who once lacked confidence become the ones who help others. They see a kid being bullied, and instead of standing by, they step in. They don't look for fights, but they refuse to let others be mistreated.

This is the kind of strength that changes the world.

The Qualities of a True Protector

They Look Out for Others – They don't just focus on themselves; they pay attention to who might need help.

They Stand Up to Bullies, Even When It's Hard – It takes courage to defend someone else, but real strength is using your voice for good.

They Set the Example – They don't just talk about doing the right thing—they do it, and others follow.

They Stay Aware and Ready – The best protectors aren't just strong—they're smart. They know what's happening around them at all times and position themselves to keep themselves and others safe.

Awareness: The First Step to Protection

The best fight is the one you never have to be in. Being a protector starts with awareness.

Know who and what is around you at all times – My sons learned this from an early age. They don't look for trouble, but they don't let trouble sneak up on them either. Whether in a crowded place or walking down the street, they know their surroundings.

Keep yourself in a position to see everything – Never let people get into your blind spots. If you're sitting in a restaurant, position yourself where you can see the exits. If you're in a group, be aware of who is behind you.

Don't let anyone come between you and your loved ones – If you're walking with family or friends, put yourself between them and the unknown, especially in uncertain situations.

Open doors for others—not just out of politeness, but for awareness – When you open a door for someone, it gives you a moment to glance inside and scan the room before stepping in.

Little habits like this become second nature and keep you ahead of potential dangers.

Trust your instincts – If something feels off, don't ignore it. Awareness and action work together—knowing what's happening is only useful if you're willing to act on it.

Strength in Silence

A true protector doesn't boast. They don't need to tell people how tough they are. The ones who talk the most are usually the weakest.

The real warriors, the real leaders, don't waste time proving themselves. They let their actions speak. They train, they prepare, and when the time comes, they do what's necessary.

A protector doesn't seek trouble, but when trouble comes, they are ready.

Parent's Guide: Raising Kids Who Protect Others

If you want your child to grow into someone who stands up for others, here's what you can do:

Encourage Empathy – Talk about how others feel. Ask, "How would you feel if that happened to you?"

Praise Acts of Kindness and Courage – Let them know that standing up for others is a sign of true strength.

Give Them the Tools to Intervene – Teach them how to step in safely—sometimes just saying, "Hey, leave him alone," is enough to stop a bully.

Teach Situational Awareness – Help them develop the habit of paying attention to their surroundings. Ask them questions like, "Who was sitting near the exit?" or "Did you notice anything unusual in that store?" to make awareness second nature.

Model the Protector Mindset – Kids learn by watching. If they see you looking out for others, staying aware, and handling situations calmly, they'll follow your lead.

We're not just teaching kids to protect themselves—we're teaching them to become protectors. That's how we create a better future.

Bonus Chapter: Lessons From the Mat and Real-Life Stories

Master Your Mind, Master the Fight

All the skill in the world can't save you if your mind is weak. Learning the physical side of fighting is easy if you have the mental toughness to handle it. That's why, in our class, we focus on the mental first—because once your mind is strong, the physical part becomes fun.

The key to winning isn't just throwing punches—it's staying calm. If you don't panic in a stressful situation, you can defeat a better fighter if he's weak-minded. I've seen it happen over and over.

I've been the underdog more times than I can count. The one thing that gave me an edge? Nothing to lose. That mindset freed me. I could ignore expectations, silence the pressure, and just fight my fight. And that's when I performed my best.

Whenever I let the outside noise get to me—when I let pressure or doubt creep in—I made mistakes. I reacted poorly. I looked uncomfortable. But when I blocked out the distractions and focused only on the task at hand, I was a force.

Life is exactly like a fight. Your mind is either working for you or against you. You have to train it to focus on what matters, block out what doesn't, and live your life—not someone else's. The only person you should compare yourself to is who you were yesterday. That's how you keep moving forward.

When you stop comparing yourself to others, jealousy, resentment, and insecurity start to fade. Instead of being quick to judge, lean toward kindness. Instead of reacting with fear or anger, take control of your emotions.

Testimonials

"I'm so appreciative of the work you all are doing. It's making such a huge impact on Calyer, on many. Impulse control, self-esteem, and the opportunity to grow those qualities in such a positive environment. Thank you both for also recognizing the whole-child perspective. So many awesome counseling/therapy, mental health strategies that you all are incorporating within your program."

-Karmen S.

"There's a guy in town named Justin Kelly . There's a kid in town named Corbin Kelly .Without them, I'm not where I am now with my health and fitness. Without them, excuses and and self lies would have won a long time ago. Thank you guys for helping me follow the right path and believing that I can be more than I ever let myself believe possible."

-Bill F.

"A little kindness
recognition..
Landon offered his arm
and stability to his Nanny
while walking on the
slippery sidewalk. Nobody
had to ask him, he just
hopped out of the truck
and helped her out. It takes
a village to raise
strong-honorable men,.
Thank you to Wes and
Justin for being a guiding
force."

-Kelly M.

Closing Message
The Mission of This Book

If you've made it this far, thank you. This book wasn't just about self-defense. It was about raising stronger, more confident kids who can handle the challenges life throws at them.

The lessons inside are more than just techniques—they're a way of life. They teach kids to:

Face fear with courage. Fear is natural, but it doesn't have to control them. Strength comes from learning to act despite fear.

Stand up for what's right. Whether defending themselves, a friend, or a stranger, true character is revealed in moments of challenge.

Lead with strength and humility. The strongest people don't have to prove it. They lead by example, helping others without needing recognition.

Be the protectors, not the victims. Confidence, awareness, and the right mindset turn kids into leaders—into people who shape the world instead of being shaped by it.

This mission doesn't stop with this book. It continues with you. Every conversation, every lesson, and every moment you spend helping a child grow stronger adds to this purpose.

If even one lesson from this book sticks with a child and makes a difference in their life, then it was worth writing.

Thank you for being part of this mission. Let's keep raising strong, confident, and bully-proof kids.

About the Author

Justin Kelly is a coach and trainer of martial arts with his own family-oriented school for training others to master themselves and become leaders, which he runs out of Carrollton, MO. He is also the founder of The Bully-Proof Project. Justin is an author, a husband, and the father of two sons.

Learn more and connect with Justin on Facebook at: *facebook.com/jekelly979*

or on his website at: *bullyproofproject.org.*

Thank You

Thank you so much for reading *Bully-Proof.* If this book impacted you, would you leave your honest thoughts as a review on the book page? And, if you know someone who could benefit, would you share it with them? It helps us reach even more people and impact more lives to create a more resilient world.

www.ingramcontent.com/pod-product-compliance
Lightning Source LLC
Chambersburg PA
CBHW071215120626

46546CB00006B/2566